Going

Back

Forward

The Dark Ages of Modern Society

By
William Blacksmith

©2014

We are entering into another round of elections and the rhetoric is heating up. I find it hard to watch political ads because more often than not, they are attacks on the other person. I do not find much substance being aired, only to say that this candidate would do the opposite of that one-which says nothing. This particular work embodies some of my thoughts as to the way we are going as a society, both good and bad. The hate-mongering is particularly bothersome. For we, are supposed to be a progressive society...thus the title.

For that reason I'm dedicating this book to the grandchildren of the world. Hopefully you can un-stupid our stupidity before we destroy the Earth.

Unofficial Ballot

Going Back Forward

Rudderless

Just Getting Old

Words and Fists

Someone Else's Storm

The Blackout

The Forest

Forever Zen

Riding In

Those Eyes

Same Again

Best Wishes

The Seer

Halloween, 2014

Mountain Stream

The Drawbridge

Youth

Zombies of Wall Street

Pasole' Weather

Night Visits

Honey Pot

Empty Cart

Didn't Know the Half of it

Cherry Tree

The Door

Lost Souls

Rubber Cup

What are You Taking?

In Flight

Marginalized

Underwear

Dating 2040

A Tip of the Hat

House on the Hill

Nap Weather

Hell's Fury

Spear of Life

The Gunfight

Upside-Down

Respect Yourself

While Nature Watches

The Some of Their Fears

Doubt

All the Money

I Shat Some Scat

Coming Out Clean

Correctness

Sunrise

Magic

Changing of the Guard

To the Good Life

Going Back Forward

Ha! The direction is moot
From the sequined bikini top
To the hem of that old
Moth-eaten Santa suit
In the fog of the roundhouse
Where they tell us we're daft
And they're spending the money
Like we're going to run out
In the halls of great reason
They wander and ponder who
Shall be received of their aura, but
Only in the right season

We're going back forward
Getting more further than toward
Coming together, just to
Come apart
We're going fast nowhere
Says the speaker of the high-chair
And we'd better be getting generous
If we're needing to start

Ha! The decision's been made
If we want anything to happen-
Anything at all, we'll
Just have to wait...

A ship will remain motionless unless something churns up the water…

Rudderless

You said that you would take me
No matter what got in the way
You led me to believe you'd respect me
No matter what I had to say
I thought that I could live with you
If you just gave me my space
Now, I'm out here on my own, on
This gray and cloudy day

Don't let me drown
Going down, I swear I did my best
Drifting to sea, please
Don't put me to this test
Without a straight path home
I'm just rudderless

The foam's along the shoreline now
So I'm leaning off the rail
I'm nervous of the coming storm
And yes, afraid to fail
You said that you would guide me
Steer me by the stars, but
We got lost along the way
Marooned, and off the charts

Going down, I know I've done my best
Without a clear path home
I'm just rudderless…

Just Getting Old

Pointed my car toward Las Vegas
To break bread with a friend from long past
Who was playing a club off the strip
And heard tell he was fading quite fast
Don't know why I sat in the back
Don't know why I felt such a fret, but
That familiar voice echoed the room, filled
With rye and lifelong regret

He stood alone at the end of the stage
People were crying about the songs that he played
Only one reason I could see that he stayed
Just when you're losing and starting to fold
Even while the world's growing so cold, he
Sang, "Honey, Just getting old"

A handful of people were listening
And clapped at their own favorite songs
I was sipping my drink with my head down
Wondering why it had been oh, so long
He shielded his eyes from the spotlight
Then motioned me to the small stage
And I would have gone to the end of the world
As-long-as he continued to play

Funny how this life will wrinkle your face
All that attention and still out of place
Nowhere to go to get out of the way
But just when you're thinking this is the road
That takes you to where you want to go, you
Hear, "Honey, Just getting old"...

<u>Words and Fists</u>

Words hit as hard as fists sometimes
They leave bruises and dents, in places
You never quite find
You can't pound your way out of a
Difficult spot
And you can't make your point
With a parting shot
Words hit hard as fists sometimes

Fists leave marks that just won't heal
Someone you know and trust, just made
It all real
You can't take it back once it's out
Should have seen it with that first doubt
Fists leave marks that just won't heal

Can't help with the reaction
It was bound to rear its head
Now, it's someone's satisfaction
To leave you for dead
Could have seen it coming, may be
But who would think it would be
Like this?
Sometimes they're much too charming
Words and fists

Words hit hard as fists sometimes
Just when you think you have it figured out
You've got to read between the lines
And it's still not fair
Each and every time…

Someone Else's Storm

This
Was someone else's storm
Someone else's gray cloud
That hung around
And you,
Caught without an umbrella
Getting rained on
Shivering in the cold
The strongest storms come
Without warning
And send a lightning bolt
Right down your spine
Just when you think, the
Tornado's finally passing
It loops around the canyon
In your mind
Don't
Fear someone else's storm
Brace yourself against
The blowing debris
Because this
Is someone else's storm
Cross the road into clearer skies
While the misery
Moves on…

**If I have any reaction to your supposition it will be
unmitigated calculated risk…**

The Blackout

The lights went out in market square
Because they didn't pay the bill
They were breaking windows over there
Some for profit
Some for thrill
Lost souls gathered on the beachhead
Counting up the stacks
Reading printouts before bed
Some professional
Some were hacks
There came crying from the blackout
All the wine had turned to salt
They danced in feathered boas
Some in innocence
Some with fault
And the flesh-peddlers were selling
But no one had change to buy
The morning bell was yet knelling
Some were wet
Some were dry
The lights went out in market square
The rats all fled the cage
They followed the tuxedos to the affair
Some were new
Some were made
We watched it all slow unfold
And the juice just drained away
The blackout's damage was untold
Some were different
Still, some remain unchanged…

The Forest

Pine needles crackled under foot
Curious four-legged creatures sniffing
Noses in the new-moist earth
Hoping to hit on a grub
A family of owls gathers on a high
Branch
Drying their feathers in the breeze
They wait for the mice, or
May be the squirrels to come out
And play
In its serenity
The forest does beckon
Moss, and the stately old trees
Birds flutter in-and-out of the bush
Taking their fill of wild blueberries
And the snake zigzags
Leaving an undefinable trail
Over-and-under the freshly fallen
Leaves
Such golden majesty!
As the sunlight spears the treetops
Then falls in shards to the ground
In its humbleness
The forest does beckon
The balance of all things being kept
By the sometimes harsh reality
Does the skunk, or the beaver
Think it beautiful?
There is nothing that says
A thicket or a dam
Is not a home...

Forever Zen

Peel and peek
For the pinpoint of light
At the edge of the horizon
Was
Flowing robes, obscuring
The sun
Become to become
Become to be one
Peel the veil
That clouds any reason
Drifting out with every breath
Beyond the obstacle, of
Physical death
Become to become
Become to be one
Ultimately
Forever Zen...

Riding In

High up on the mesa
Over-looking the sand
Two hawks spiraled down
Towards the Rio Grande
Showing me the path
Showing me the way
Riding in east, at
The end of the day
Riding in for the night, after
Looking for strays...

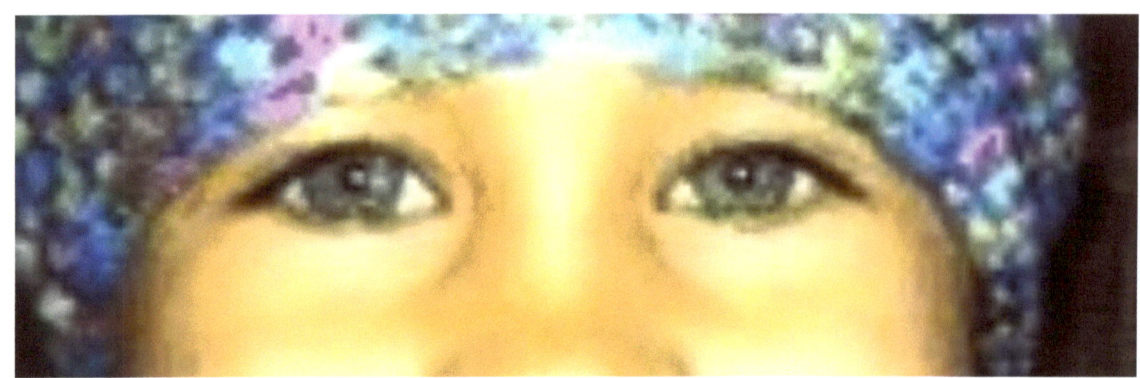

<u>Those Eyes</u>

Those eyes
Look at the world in amazement
In innocence
They watch the rain come down
See the cars go by
They tear
At an injustice, or injury
They blink
To wipe the sleep away
Those eyes
So much like your mama
Sometimes questioning, sometimes
Answering
So many emotions
Happiness, confusion, suspicion
Empathy, sympathy, guilt
Even sorrow and pride
So much of life seen, in
So little time
Through those eyes...

You cannot feed a nation with weapons of war...

Same Again

Burn the old idols
They say
Chisel the fairies and sprites
Off of the cavern walls
Erase
All mention of Akhenaton
We have hanged our own
Witches in the short past
A new crusade begun
The Ottomans
And the Christians at it
Again
What makes this tablet
Heretical?
Or, that one truth-
Other than us saying?
Heaven and hell
That's where souls go, when
They don't know where
To go
And we relive with viciousness
So for our words
So for their actions
So little responsible reaction
Cut down the ancients
They say
From the cedars of Lebanon
To Disneyland
Pointing to the west
To the lands of sin, and
Debauchery
While they sell their women...

Best Wishes

No granted wish comes
Without an addendum, a
Reciprocity clause
From the bearer to the
Bearee
So, wish wisely, and
Try to go unpunished
No shooting star
Crosses a path without
The burn
It will take its magic
Fairy dust elsewhere, before
Giving in to a
Non-believer, who
Takes that for granted…

The Seer

There must have been one, who
Has seen what has come to pass, all
The death and destruction, the inequity
The unfairness
One that has gazed into the crystal
Pulled the sequential tarot cards
Read the bones
What has been seen through the smoke
Of the sage bundle
Is a most uncertain future, for
Replaying the past…

Halloween, 2014

The skies blackened, they cried
But only on one side of the street
While totally avoiding the other
Screams, oh there were screams, as
The hammer never touched down, pitting
Father against mother
Sister against brother
The requiem mass hadn't yet played
Still waiting for the dark ones to show
Evisceration was there for the asking, from
The frocked used-car salesmen
All clamoring for the devil's soul

Sanity had been thrown in the pit
The glad-hander was paired with, the
Southernmost witch
And sparks continued to fly
Until the air smelt of sulphur and lye

Lust's faded fortunes, they rot
Greying what was once so green
The color of well-paid for spoil
Nightmare upon eternal nightmare, shows
What the future may become, red
The blood of saints
The river's boil
A bayonet is not a baton
To be wielded by the unholy few
Greed for flesh rears its head, for some
High-pitched in the reeds, on
The strong witch's brew...

Mountain Stream

How far back into the mountains
Do you go?
Twist and wind around crags and
Through valleys you flow
Maeander over the fall and winter
Torrent through the spring, only
To dry to a trickle through
The summer
A good snow-pack could get
You down to the gulf
Pregnant with fishes and all
Sorts of river wildlife
I'll bet you've seen some amazing
Sunsets along your journey
And awe inspiring sunrises on
Your long trip home
Long-held secrets rarely break free
To ride with the current
Your mouth may be open but
You do not give them up
Stay pristine and unfettered, stay
True to your purpose…

The Drawbridge

Infidels, stormed the castle
Shooting balls of fire towards
The ramparts
As the king and his court
Were spirited out the back
We set the moat alight, hoping
To burn their unholy colors
And a brave soul or two
Withstood the molten tar, to
Rappel the outer wall
The village knaves hoarded
The gold together
And threw it down the nearest
Artesian well
The drawbridge had been stuck
Half-up
Man-upon-man added his weight
Attempting to seal it shut
Infidels, were on the grounds
Now, coming in dismembered
Columns
Arrows flew in no particular
Direction, hitting both
Friend and foe
Traitors, turncoats, the foreign
Hoard came strong
Not a man, woman, child saved
And the gold found out
The king, meanwhile
Plotted his dared revenge, only
To keep the battle
Alive…

Youth

When I was young
It was Viet Nam
Free love, LSD, the Watts riots
Black Panthers, Moonies
Jim Jones
We had Woodstock, and
Haight Ashbury
Mama Cass, Jimmy, and
Janice
We had the Weather Underground
The Chicago Seven, and
Dr. Martin Luther King
People burned their Draft Cards
Ran naked through the parks
When I was young
We listened to our elders, (mostly)
But were also disciplined
At home, at school
Then
We fell into responsibility
Jobs, sex, drugs, money
Homelessness
We cared for Civil Rights
We didn't care at all
We had faith, and love, and
Adultery and divorce
We buried our fair share
Of Star Children
What's changed from then
Until now?
Nothing at all...

Zombies of Wall Street

Volley, all your paper bombs
Try to get the stuck ones free
Yet the muck has them sunken
Without a tell
Without a read
Still they mull around the circle
Crumpled carbons to keep warm
The time of trading at its end
No issues sold, without
Proper form
Who amongst you climbs atop
To intake a breath of heady air?
While those below cannot untwine
They've lost will
They've lost the care
Drown in your distilled spirits
The taxi out just costs a beer
For eating the souls of innocents
Have it all
Keep it near
Gather at the feet of master, who
Burns money for the hell-of-it
He seems to have you in his power
He'll give you life
But just a little bit
Enter zombies of Wall Street
New converts forming every day
Admission is never-ever free, what
That price is
We just can't say…

A pound of flesh for an ounce of soul seems like a rip-off…

Pasole' Weather

The smells that come out of the
Kitchen
About this time of year
When a chill starts to ride with
The canyon winds
Another log on the fire, my dear
In-between the wood pellets, and
Piñón smoke
The chili's beginning to blend
The magnificent waft fills the
Neighborhood
From start to end
It's Pasole' weather again
The home team is playing in town
People are baking, and
Raking the coals
To get that season's last barbeque
Down
Swamp-coolers are covered
And the pork roast's in the pot
A hint of garlic and oregano
As the stove flames
And gets hot
Somebody's ready with butter
And tortilla
At the other end of the table
Honey and sopapilla
You'd think
With a large pot it would last
But that is the nature of weather
And Pasole'
Neither one lasts…

<u>Night Visits</u>

The brilliant light lasting only
A moment
Of the color never perceived
Disappeared near the bedroom
Window
Cracked open ever so slightly
Came the hint of smoke and vinegar
Not the first time
Held strong to the bed
And swear that the eyes are open
Looking straight
At the moving shadows on the
Wall
Not the first time
Incisions and pain, felt
As punishment for past-life regrets
Atonement for imagined
Wrong-doing
Still, the muffled murmurs
Resist most detection
Only letting through enough
To keep the senses tuned
Anyone else
Would have been sent to the ward
Not those that can, keep
This secret
The brilliant light moving
Quickly away
Though, glad for the freedom of
Movement and breath, feels
Strangely empty…

Honey Pot

Hot honey
Dripping from the walls, of
Your inner sanctum
Busy little bee
Making big deposits
Loads of pollen, and nectar
All that friction
Thickens things
Inside the honey pot
It can be thick
And slick
At the same time
Sweet, sweet scent
Rising from the flower field
A primal attraction
To carry the source, to
The seed
To gather up what
Can be hardly toted-
Is a matter of greed
Hot honey
How has it shaped your
Comb?
In time it fills, then
Seeps back out
Still tingling, from an
Ill-placed stinger
And the walls tremble
With the bee's buzz
That which
Revels in nature, creates
Perfection...

Empty Cart

Looks like the line's moving slowly
May be they'll open up another soon
Doesn't make a difference, much
Seeing the empty cart ahead of me
Looks like the checkers have no interest
Wonder what goes on in their minds
Probably see all this stuff for sale
And worrying about the evening meal
How'd we get to this point here?
It's never been exactly clear
Economics has not been my strong suit
But as we get further behind
There are finer things that come to mind
And I'd give every single one, of them
The boot
This one's gone and bought another yacht
Hopefully gets lost out at sea
The tabloids in the aisle make me sick
All the excess and my empty cart
Looks like we're finally up to pay
I can see the kids becoming agitated
Rubbing ten's together doesn't make
Them propagate
I could just walk out but didn't
Have the heart
When'd we get to this point now?
We'd like to get ahead, but how?
The cart was so much fuller in my youth
It will be gone before tomorrow comes
Hard times can make a family numb
Every tale of woe has a seed of truth…

Didn't Know the Half of it

The glass is half-empty, yes
That may be pessimistic
Still, wander around this town
And see if it doesn't get you
Down
There are missiles in the mountain
And the coins are gone from
The fountain
Didn't mean to take a single hit
But, didn't know the half of it
Now,
Every side has something to say
White noise on the TV everyday
We'll prop you up
We'll help the poor
We'll decide who's in
Then we'll make more
Decisions that take your money
But not your pain
The glass is half-empty, still
May be that's a blessing
The only way to go is up
How can anyone think they
Have it rough?
There are drones on the horizon
Something to keep your eyes on
What do you mean, you
Didn't vote for this, you
Just don't know the half of it...

It's not that difficult to liken the state to the pervert neighbor kid looking in the bedroom window...

Cherry Tree

Did you get your fruit from
The cherry tree?
Or, was it already a raisin?
Was it ripe and plump
In season to pick?
Or, were you afraid to?
The orchard owner keeps
A good eye
On his new fresh crop
The younger trees have not
Flowered yet, but will-
Bottom to top
Are you collecting stems from
The cherry tree?
Or, will one be enough?
Working toward the cherry pit
Is sometimes
Long and tough
While the orchard owner
Is out of sight
You make your basket ready
And the cherry tree won't
Shake too much
If your hands are steady
Did you get your fruit from
The cherry tree, or
Was the fruit already gone?
The tree may have been picked
Clean before
Then you just move on...

The Door

There's a door, that
Everybody walks through
It's called, "Experience"
Some may hesitate, by
The entrance
Not knowing what's in store
And the other side
Isn't any easier
There will be a few going
In time-and-time again
You would think this portal
Leads into the sunshine
But this is where the dark
Begins and ends
There's a door, that
A lot of us are afraid of
Still
It calls to me and you
One step across the threshold
Looking both ways besides
And this squeaking door
Makes the heart pound
You want to take it once, and
Be on the path
But beyond this one there's
A thousand others
And it's hard to keep your bearings
Where you're at
There's a door
That everybody knocks on
It's called, "Experience"...

Lost Souls

Nearly all graveyards
Throughout the millennia, have
Been lost
Dug up, rearranged, flooded out
Buried deeper still
The phantoms and phantasms
Lost in their final rest
Forever to search the countryside
To find a bed to lay
Ectoplasmic sheep in hunt
For a Shepard
Take care to build a house
Or erect another parking garage
For, they've been known
To walk through walls, at
The worst of times
Take care and give them space
Be wary the hitch-hiker
Pale in the blood moonlight
Lest, you find yourself a journey
That never ends...

Rubber Cup

Rubber cup
Let there be no pinhole
No seepage
The last line of defense
Before the weeping
Smothered in fine jelly
To stop a growing belly...

What are you Taking?

What are you taking with you
Now that your journey has begun?
The box is lowering, the
Ashes spread into the wind
Your fame, your money, your
Accolades
What will start you on your path-
When all the fluids are gone, and
You're left an empty bag?
Gold, and spices, and beloved pets
Only occupy the space
You may have to work your way
Up to the bottom
After what you just left behind
Came in with nothing, leaving
The same
Common sense is never that kind
What are you taking with you
Now that the slate has been wiped
Clean?
There are maggots above ground
As-well-as below
Either way, you're totally free
Now more burdens to carry, no
More deadbeats to ferry
No more banks or trust funds
To molest
Just quiet, peaceful darkness
For a well-deserved rest...

I guess you can always get buried in your car...

In Flight

Are you looking at the world
From the ground, or the air?
Is your sense of perspective, up
Here or down there?
High up on the mesa we
Anxiously wait
For the sunrise to show us
An incredible state
Hot-air balloons, ballooning
As-far-as can be seen
A myriad of colors, yellows
Blues, and greens
Are you looking at the world
Now
With the same set of eyes?
Look up, look up, look up, you'll
Be pleasantly surprised...

Marginalized

We are not born to hate
We are not born to victimize
Or marginalize
They are not inherited traits
Not like having brown eyes, or
Black hair
We are not born to prefer
One gender over the next, nor
Chosen a lover right out of the womb
These are taught crimes
These are thought crimes
One person or ideal, is just
As valid as the observer's, but
For the little voice of righteousness
And morality
Whispering in your ear
Blasting over the air-waves
Pounding on the pulpit
Where the bane of authority, tells
One that the other's bad, decrepit,
Degenerate, leaching
The sword of common sense, of
Level-headedness
Knows in itself that "different"
Isn't unjust, immoral, or evil, it's
Just different, and
There's nothing to fear…

People who are forever showing the world that they are strong in their beliefs-to the point of injustice and violence, are our weakest links…

Underwear

What deep secrets are you hiding?
Your portrayal on the surface, can
Be misread
Would it be cruel to ask about
Any of your desires?
We'll put two-and-two together
Easy enough, instead
Really, it's never been about sexuality
What's put in or put out is not the thing
What scares some people is who you
"Love"
And who you don't
It's fascinating to know which way you
Swing
What are you wearing under there?
The cameras didn't quite catch
Your chosen style
Would it be vain for us to ask you
To bare it to the public?
Since we really, really, really like
The way you smile
Simply, we're amazed by difference
But on the outside who can tell?
May be the biggest fear we have is letting
People in
Because then they'd see we've had
These fantasies ourselves…

**Are our lives so dull and boring that we need to
sensationalize the lives of others?…**

Dating 2040

I'm going to pick you up, in my
Magno-levitating car
Heading to the fly-in on Mars
We're going to dance the night
Away
In zero-gravity
Because the universe is ours

Funny how, yesterday we were tweaking
And our elders, like all elders, were freaking
Now we'll settle for green tea, and
Antiquing
What were we thinking when we were young?

I'm going to set you down, right
In front of the door
Looks like we may be here on time
We could have led each other
Astray
In zero-gravity
Somehow we always toed the line

Funny, yesterday we left from Albuquerque
Full of life, alive and perky
Now we might as well settle for
Tofurkey
What did we think we'd have when
We were done?
What were we thinking? We were never
That young...

A Tip of the Hat

Old friend
We've taken many different paths
Together
Basked in the sun, and
Withstood the bad weather
Even now, it's hard
To see you moving on
Old friend
When you look back at those
Happy times
I won't see your face, but
Know you're smiling
Just remember inside, you're
Never gone
You may be leaving something behind
For the chance to find what you can find
When you look into tomorrow
See the opportunity
To finally free your mind
And we'll surely miss your presence here
The one of us who made it all
So clear
When we look into tomorrow, realize
That we still hold you dear
Old friend
You must take this path yourself
Make new memories, and
Have fun if nothing else
We might catch our senses, a time
Or two
Look around and see you
Moving on...

House on the Hill

We moved in to the house on the hill
November, two-thousand ten
Vowing to leave this poverty behind us
Never to go back there again
Rising up from life's early ashes
We gathered the brood and set out
And canvassed one end of the state to the
Other
Just to ease anyone's doubt
We drove up nonchalant to the house on the hill
Certainly entitled to this new address
Parked the oil-burner deep in the garage
In case someone had the need for redress
Oh,
Just look how far we've come
With floors, and windows, and drapes
From the café-slash-bar in the city, to a
Personal chef serving crepes
Our first dinner party at the house on the hill
What a glorious event, with
All of the relatives safely out-of-town
There are just things we try hard to prevent
Showing off our new found lot
A black-tie affair to be honestly sure
If you did not receive an invitation, obviously
You didn't pay for the tour
Really, once we get settled in
Comfortable, we won't ever be leaving
And we'll thank, then pay back in kind, all
The gifts we are receiving...

Nap Weather

Odd serenity
Dark and breezy mysterious shroud
Cloaked against the mountains
At once a gray/black cloud
The tingle of tender raindrops, soothe
A wide variety of ills
Whisper quiet as the spinning stills
Ah, then the noises hush
Nothing above but circled avian, dropping
Into the underbrush
Great thoughts
Are mounted in the wandering mind
This is to sleep, or half to sleep, while
The electric field unwinds
It is best released from the tether
To float endlessly like a feather
Arms crossed under the chin, just
To enjoy the weather…

Hell's Fury

Not one person living, can go beyond
The written word
They take it as the literal truth, and
Outwardly preach to its supremacy
Inward, thinking
The most heinous, vile things
Their devils and demons laughing
Hysterically
As the lemmings near the bridge
And somebody asks for a match…

Those of you waiting for the rapture may take some comfort in the fact that nature will turn us into kindling first...

If I have any regret, it's that hesitation negated most of the things I'd be regretful for...

Spear of Life

Spear of life, strike true!
Find your mark, and make the wound
Peel back the flesh
Feel its dew
Spear of life, strike straight!
Your tip has knocked on many a gate
At your gleaming sight
They capitulate
And the gashes it leaves behind
Still aching
A father's seething wrath, a
Mother's heart breaking
Nothing told of origins or how
It's made
The only full authority is the
Hand that guides the blade
Spear of life, strike kind!
For in the end one scabbard will
Calm your head, and
Ease your mind...

The Gunfight

Two O' Clock
I came from the barbershop
He, one-hundred paces ahead
We faced
No words between us, just
A slight against one or the other
This, the result
Eye-to-eye in a frown
No wind, no sound, just the
Dust kicked up from our boots
We each had routine
I, flexing my fingers, cracking
Knuckles
He, shaking off the night's drink
Waving his hand over
The hammer
And the guns un-skinned
And the aims were true
The "pops" coming well after
The trigger
Was it one bullet, or six, I
Cannot remember
We stood looking ahead for
A long second
Then, I saw him fall, crumpled
In a heap
That was the last thing
I saw...

It's really survival of the most adaptable...

Upside-Down

When the world turns upside-down
When the rivers and oceans engulf, all
That we've made
When the earth shakes and crumbles
The great monuments
When the ants and the roaches chew
Up the rest
When the world turns upside-down
When the magma moves up, to
Swallow and eat its fill
When the moon is knocked from orbit
When the arctic winter cloaks the
Earth
There will be no governments
There will be no religion
There will be no art, nor culture
There will be no hands, or ropes, or
Lifeboats
There will be no sympathy
There will be no leaders, there
Will be no followers
There will be no lofty dead, or
Ingratiating principles
There will be no holy, nor unholy
There will be no words from the sky
There will be no law, or justice
There will be no trees, no vegetation
There will be no meat on the hoof
There will be no fish in the ocean
All that will be
Is the collective consciousness
That should have known better...

Respect Yourself

Paint dries
Faster than attitudes change
Always someone to kick you down
To harass and antagonize
To keep you down
And disrespect rolls along the
Ground
Picking up hatred, giving it weight
Until even hate is unrecognizable
As hate
They disrespect your gender
They disrespect your love
Whether you're for the war, or
Against
Whether you're hugging trees, or
Burning trash
Respect yourself, screw
Everybody else
Words fly
Across the chambers of reason
Labels hurt more than help
It's how you cope, not how loud
You yell
And to give respect lifts the
Lowest soul
Who you've encouraged, gave some
Love
Says just how you roll
Respect yourself, screw
Everybody else that shows no
Respect...

I am sometimes rendered mute, wearing a vagina as a mask…

When we've come to the point where the planet houses nothing but rich, white, heterosexual males-we will have succeeded in creating hell…

It doesn't matter what you call yourself in the end. Everyone believes what they <u>need</u> to believe…

<u>While Nature Watches</u>

"There's enough to go around"
They once said
Live off the land, reap from
The breadbasket
And have a lot of little mouths
To feed
To help to work the land
Well we don't plant anymore
And we don't sow anymore
And we don't farm anymore
But we still like to make babies
Then blame it on, "God's Plan"
While they're strip-mining the
Mountains
And killing the water
And warring over resources
That won't matter much
Underwater…

The Some of Their Fears

Can't hear the sabers rattling
Over expert commentary
The bylines and the headlines
Scream on deaf ears
Yet we can still see the captions
About the newest assault
Invasions of mind and body
They're coming across the borders
Suicide bombers, with
Dirty needles
To inject us with holiness
To blast our skin with flame-throwers
Melt away the hard-candy shell
And everyone's got a mouthpiece
Condemning this, accepting that
Putting the fear into fear
For the already afraid
If you sat next to a turban
Ran your car out of gas
Took a bite from someone's sandwich
Or,
Visited Texas anytime (at all)
Might as well pack your bags, for
Valhalla
We heard it on the news
In every righteous politico-rant
They're coming for our guns, our
Money, and our young
Still wonder, how many took that
Note
And bothered to vote…

Doubt

These are the things
That make you believe
In things that you've never
Believed in
These are the bugs
That crawl in the flesh
The ones no one can see, but
They're felt any way
And that smell in the room
Might be brimstone
Or, rosemary depending
On the sin
There are yet skeptics
No matter what they're given
Cannot
And will not be swayed
There is no truth
To so-called free will
If not unseen forces, then
Humans have done
There is no need
To preserve Mother Earth
If paradise has already
Been promised
These are the things
That make you deny
What has been placed in front
Of you once
And that smell in the room
Is you, crapping your pants
After finally being
Honest...

You swept me up in your orbit, now your warmth is my neighborhood...

All the Money

All the money in the world
Won't save you from yourself
It might make you happy
(For a while)
And build you that bomb-shelter
And get you the vote
But it cannot change destiny
It cannot re-route karma
All the money you can carry
Will mean nothing after death
Enjoy it while you can
So spend it, invest it, lose it,
Pass it on
Light your cigars with it
Remember,
You can't eat gold, and
You can't drink oil
When the fight becomes, for
Water and food
Even the highest cultured
Icons tend to be savage
Amazing how much more
Money is used for harm, than
Good
All the money in the world
Is for naught...

I Shat Some Scat

There I was
Secured on the throne of thought
Ensconced on the seat of power
Relegated to the dunce's chair
Alone with my mind
Sponging up the news of the day
Figuring
For a moment
How to save all the ills befalling
I thought about inventing a miracle
Cure
And if I was there, how I could
Make the political parties talk again
If I could sell this idea
We could build a car that would
Run for a year non-stop
I thought, if we just ate bamboo
No one would starve
And reproductive rights are a
Priority
I couldn't decide if either Playboy
Or Cosmo gave good advice
There I was
Wondering why there was no bidet
Thoughts are explosive
Much like sports stars and candidates
Fast, out of the gate, then nothing
I thought I might sit here
And solve world peace, but I
"poo-pooed" the idea…

Coming Out Clean

Solar cells don't belch out toxins
And they don't make the air nuclear noxious
Wind turbines don't burn fossil fuel
Or spew carbon monoxide, it's true
Why has the guano trade suffered so?
Until we burn half the rain forest, instead
Of letting it grow
As the oxygen levels go down, and
The ozone levels inch up
We shrug uncaring shoulders, "What's up?"
We've over-loaded earth with inhumanity
The same anti-control social insanity
Unlucky mother bearing a daughter
Born into enslavement or slaughter
We have wars on crime and drugs, while
Our policing is done by hired thugs
And we could extend our growing yields
But would rather fund the poppy fields
Hopefully, the next species of overlords
Won't see caring for the planet
Such a chore...

Correctness

Politicians lie, it's
In their nature
This, stretching the truth
Because the truth, if
The truth be told
Would put them out
Of business...

<u>Sunrise</u>

The sun will rise another day
How many more, we'll never know
It's not the same for all of us
Don't try to count the days
They roll into each other, for sure
All we know is it's never enough
How many dawns are there left?
Every one born is a surprise
And the morning greets a breath
Anew
Some will find the wonder of it
Some wake up on the cranky side
The lucky ones see great pleasure
In attitude
The sun will rise another day
To put the darkness out of place
And run its course across the sky
There's no need to think about it
This is not a complete race
Just one more reason for a
Contenting sigh…

Magic

The conjurer has misplaced his wand
The rabbit has escaped from his top hat
Not one more kerchief coming from his
Sleeve
His audience losing their will to believe
He spends his nights now on a
Silent stage
His assistant having traded in her tights
The smugepots are all snuffed
In a sense he couldn't be more relieved
The magic that once filled this
Amphitheater
From the orchestra to the front-door
Greeter
Is nothing but a memory in a
Haunted auditorium
The crumbling playbill said it once
And the last show had been months-
And months
Its star now living at the sanitarium
The conjurer now says forgotten lines
The fire's not in his fingertips at all
No more silver dollars pulled from
A bystander's ear
He misses how the crowd would
Cheer and cheer
He spends his days now in a padded
Room
The nurses, not being fond of his act
The floodlights all are broken
And not a dime left for Everclear
In a sense he couldn't be more relieved…

Changing of the Guard

The time is coming near
We've made no single progress
Only slung words across the fence
The troops can't rally
Behind weak leadership, or infighting
There's a bigger enemy to face
If the wars are won on the
Battlefield
Then we're certainly at stalemate
Neither foe giving ground
Fighting jungle warfare, without
A jungle
May be we should think about
The changing of the guard
As we negotiate this cease-fire
The bombs continue to fall, bombs
You know are blind to innocence
And the rhetoric has become vile,
Inarticulate and vain
We can still choose to fight for wars
Or fight for peace
The time is running out
All the players have taken the stage
In a stare-down going nowhere
The troops won't follow
Those who keep their bellies empty
While supping on the finest
Laissez faire
It really shouldn't be this hard
The changing of the guard…

To the Good Life

It's a good life
For the give and the take of it
It's a great life
And it is what you make of it
We know you have a restless soul
Take
The memories you've made
Wherever you go
To the good life
Always let the darkness see you smile
Because it's a great life
And you've brightened up our lives
If only for a while
So, keep us in mind when you roam
Where you drop your bags is your home
It's a good life
For the short and the long of it
Live a great life
There's certainly nothing wrong
With it
Always know we have your back
Whatever place in time you're at
To the good life...

Some friends arc burned into your psyche, while some are just a memory...

The End